MISSION SOLAR SYSTEM

NANCY DICKMANN

QEB

Quarto is the authority on a wide range of topics.

Quarto educates, entertains and enriches the lives of our readers—enthusiasts and lovers of hands-on living.

www.quartoknows.com

Editor: Amanda Askew
Designer: Dave Ball

First Published in 2017 by QEB Publishing,
an imprint of The Quarto Group.
6 Orchard Road, Suite 100
Lake Forest, CA 92630
T: +1 949 380 7510
F: +1 949 380 7575
www.QuartoKnows.com

A CIP record for this book is available from the Library of Congress.

ISBN 978-1-68297-376-9

Manufactured in Shenzhen, China RD102017

9 8 7 6 5 4 3 2 1

MIX
Paper from responsible sources
FSC® C101537
www.fsc.org

PICTURE CREDITS
fc=front cover, bc=back cover, t=top, b=bottom, l=left, r=right, c=center

ALAMY: 15cl Irina Dmitrienko, 50t dotted zebra, 69 John White Photos, 73b Stocktrek Images, Inc. **GETTY:** fc adventtr **NASA:** 4–5c JPL-Caltech, 5t, 5b, 7 SDO, 8t ESA/SOHO, 9cl ESA/SOHO, 9cr JAXA/PPARC, 10 SDO, 11b SDO/HMI/Goddard Space Flight Center, 12–13b Johns Hopkins University Applied Physics Laboratory/Carnegie Institution of Washington, 14t Johns Hopkins Applied Physics Laboratory/Carnegie Institution of Washington, 16 Johns Hopkins University Applied Physics Laboratory/Carnegie Institution of Washington, 17r Goddard Space Flight Center, 19cl JPL, 19cr JPL, 20 ESA/C. Carreau, 21 Goddard Space Flight Center, 22t JPL, 23b JPL-Caltech, 23c Reto Stockli/NASA Earth Observatory, 23t, 24 Goddard Space Flight Center, 25 NASA Earth Observatory/ Jesse Allen, 27 JPL/USGS, 28–28b GSFC, 29t, 30b, 31, 32l JPL-Caltech, 32b JPL-Caltech/University of Arizona, 33t JPL-Caltech/University of Arizona, 34t GSFC, 34–35 JPL-Caltech/MSSS, 35t JPL-Caltech, 36–37 JPL-Caltech/MSSS, 37t JPL-Caltech/MSSS, 40bl JPL-Caltech, 41b JPL/JHUAPL, 42b JPL-Caltech/UCLA/MPS/DLR/IDA, 42t JPL-Caltech/ UCLA/MPS/DLR/IDA, 43c JPL/DLR, 43l JPL-Caltech/SwRI, 44t JPL-Caltech, 45l ESA/ J. Nichols (University of Leicester), 45r Johns Hopkins University Applied Physics Laboratory/Southwest Research Institute, 46   JPL-Caltech/SwRI/MSSS/Betsy Asher Hall/Gervasio Robles, 47 JPL-Caltech/SwRI/MSSS/Jason Major, 48–49 JPL/Space Science Institute, 50bl JPL-Caltech/Space Science Institute, 51b JPL-Caltech/SSI/ Cornell, 51t JPL-Caltech/Space Science Institute, 52 JPL-Caltech/SSI, 53r JPL/University of Arizona/University of Idaho, 54b ESA, 54cl ESA/JPL/ University of Arizona, 55b JPL-Caltech/ASI, 56b ESA/T. Cornet, 56t ESA/JPL/University of Arizona, 57 JPL-Caltech, 59t JPL/USGS, 59b JPL, 60b   Johnson Space Center/Earth Sciences and Image Analysis Laboratory, 60c   ESA/L. Lamy (Observatory of Paris, CNRS, CNES), 61 JPL-Caltech/SETI Institute, 62t, 62b JPL, 63tl JPL/DLR, 63cl JPL/DLR, 63cr JPL/Space Science Institute, 64 JPL/Space Science Institute, 65 Johns Hopkins University Applied Physics Laboratory/Southwest Research Institute, 66t, 66b Johns Hopkins University Applied Physics Laboratory/Southwest Research Institute/Lunar and Planetary Institute, 67t ESA/M. Buie/Southwest Research Institute, 67cr Johns Hopkins University Applied Physics Laboratory/Southwest Research Institute, 68br, 68l Johns Hopkins University Applied Physics Laboratory/Southwest Research Center/Chandra X-Ray Center, 70l ESA/Rosetta/MPS for OSIRIS Team, 71t JPL, 72 ESA/Rosetta/Philae/CIVA, 75r, 76bl JPL-Caltech, 76tr JPL-Caltech, 77br ESA/ATG medialab, 77tl ESA/J. Huart **SHUTTERSTOCK:** bc Vadim Sadovski, 4–5c BlueRingMedia, 4b cigdem, 8b SkyPics Studio, 15cr SkyPics Studio, 18t Elenarts, 18bl SkyPics Studio, 22b stas11, 28bl SkyPics Studio, 39 Mopic, 41t Andrea Danti, 58cr Lauritta, 63bl Tristan3D, 70t Elenarts, 71l MarcelClemens, 74–75 Pavel Chagochkin

CONTENTS

WELCOME TO
THE SOLAR SYSTEM

The **planet** we live on—Earth—is part of the Solar System,
a "family" of planets, **asteroids**, **comets**, and other space objects,
which all travel around the Sun.

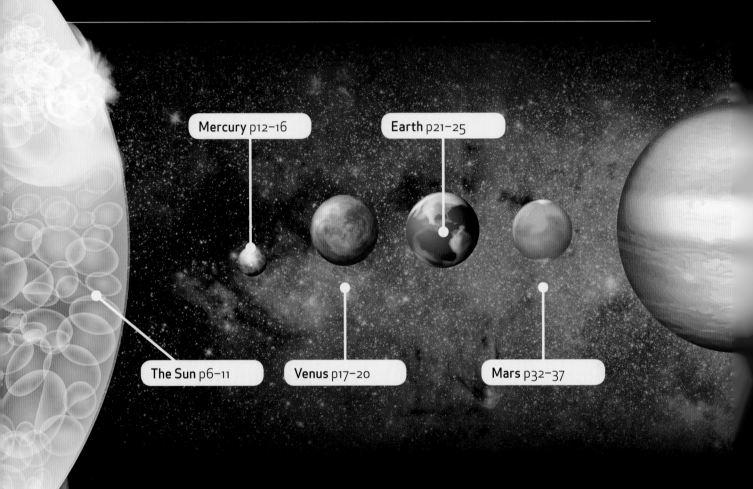

Mercury p12–16

Earth p21–25

The Sun p6–11

Venus p17–20

Mars p32–37

The planets
follow nearly
circular
paths around
the Sun.

Holding it together

The Sun is the largest object in
the Solar System. The pull of its
gravity—a force that attracts objects
to each other—holds all the objects
in the Solar System in place. Gravity
also makes these objects move, or
orbit, around the Sun.

Exploring the Solar System

The Solar System is enormous! The farthest planet, Neptune, is 2.8 billion miles from the Sun. It takes about 12 years for a spacecraft to travel that far. Astronauts have visited Earth's **Moon**, but robot spacecraft have to be used to orbit around or land on the surfaces of the other planets. We also use powerful telescopes to look into the depths of space.

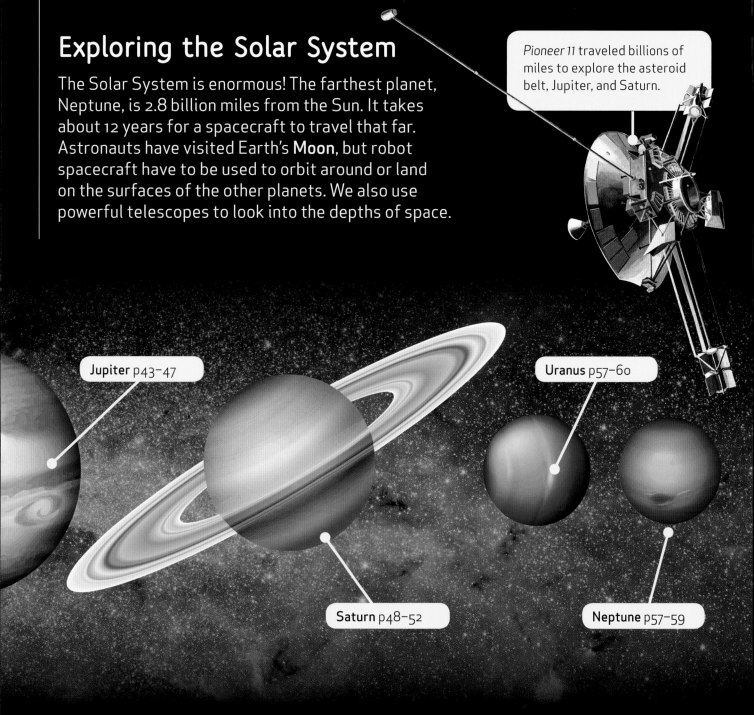

Pioneer 11 traveled billions of miles to explore the asteroid belt, Jupiter, and Saturn.

Jupiter p43–47

Uranus p57–60

Saturn p48–52

Neptune p57–59

From 1981 to 2011, there were 135 space shuttle missions.

Get ready for launch

This amazing book will take you on a tour of the Solar System. In the last 50 years, we have learned a huge amount about our neighbors in space. Each spacecraft mission brings new knowledge and stunning images. This book highlights some of the most amazing recent discoveries.

SCORCHING SUN

The Sun is the brightest object in the sky, and essential for life on Earth. We depend on its light and heat—plants use sunlight to make food, and animals eat plants for energy.

What is the Sun?

The Sun is a star—a huge ball of glowing gas. It is just one of many stars in a **galaxy** called the Milky Way. To us, it looks bigger than other stars because it is closer. It is about 93 million miles away from Earth. Although light travels faster than anything in the universe, the Sun is so far away that its light takes about eight minutes to reach us.

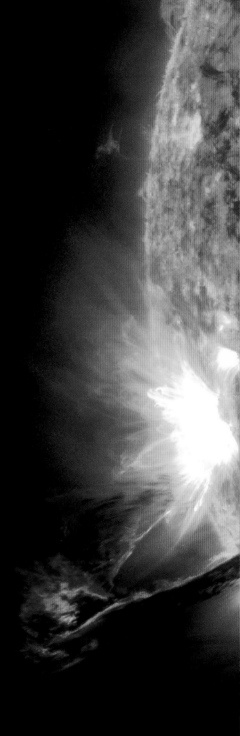

The age of the Sun

Astronomers think that the Sun formed about 4.6 billion years ago, at the same time as the rest of the Solar System. In about 5 billion years, the Sun will die because the "fuel" that burns inside it, producing heat and light energy, will run out.

The wrong way around

People once believed Earth was at the center of the universe, and everything else traveled around it. When astronomers tracked the movements of the stars and planets, they realized that their paths only made sense if the Sun were at the center of the Solar System.

The Sun is constantly active, sending bursts of energy out into space.

THE SUN:
A MISSION REPORT

3.6
million °F

AVERAGE TEMPERATURE OF
THE SUN'S OUTER LAYER,
THE CORONA

The spacecraft

Solar and Heliospheric Observatory
(*SOHO*) is about 930,000 miles
from Earth. It was launched in
1995 to study the layers of the
Sun. A second spacecraft, *Solar
Dynamics Observatory* (*SDO*), was
launched in 2010. It studies how
the Sun changes, and how those
changes affect Earth.

SOHO

What's inside the Sun?

The Sun is made up of super-hot gases
—mostly hydrogen and helium. Its **core**,
or center, is where energy is produced.
This is the hottest part, at a scorching
27 million °F! This energy moves through
the radiative and convective zones to
the outer layers—the photosphere,
chromosphere, and corona.

10,000°F

THE AVERAGE
TEMPERATURE OF
THE PHOTOSPHERE

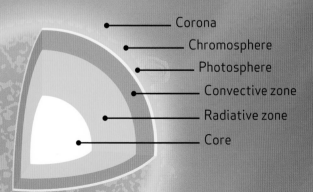

- Corona
- Chromosphere
- Photosphere
- Convective zone
- Radiative zone
- Core

Which part of the Sun do we see?

We see the outermost layer, called
the corona. It reaches for millions
of miles into space. *SOHO* is trying
to discover why the corona is so
hot. Underneath the corona is the
chromosphere. The thin surface
layer is called the photosphere.

Why does the Sun shine?

Inside the core, **atoms** of hydrogen crash into each other and stick together to form helium gas. This gives out energy that reaches Earth as heat and light. *SOHO* discovered that the Sun's core **rotates** once a week, whereas the surface rotates just once a month.

It can take one million years for energy to travel from the core to the Sun's surface.

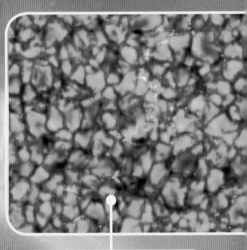

The Sun's surface has a pattern called "granulation" caused by bubbling gases.

Does the Sun change?

The Sun is constantly active. Dark patches called "**sunspots**" appear on the surface and later disappear. The number of sunspots and storms reaches a peak every 11 years. *SDO* has detected sunspots forming below the surface, before they become visible.

110 > THE NUMBER OF EARTHS THAT COULD SIT SIDE-BY-SIDE ACROSS THE WIDEST PART OF THE SUN

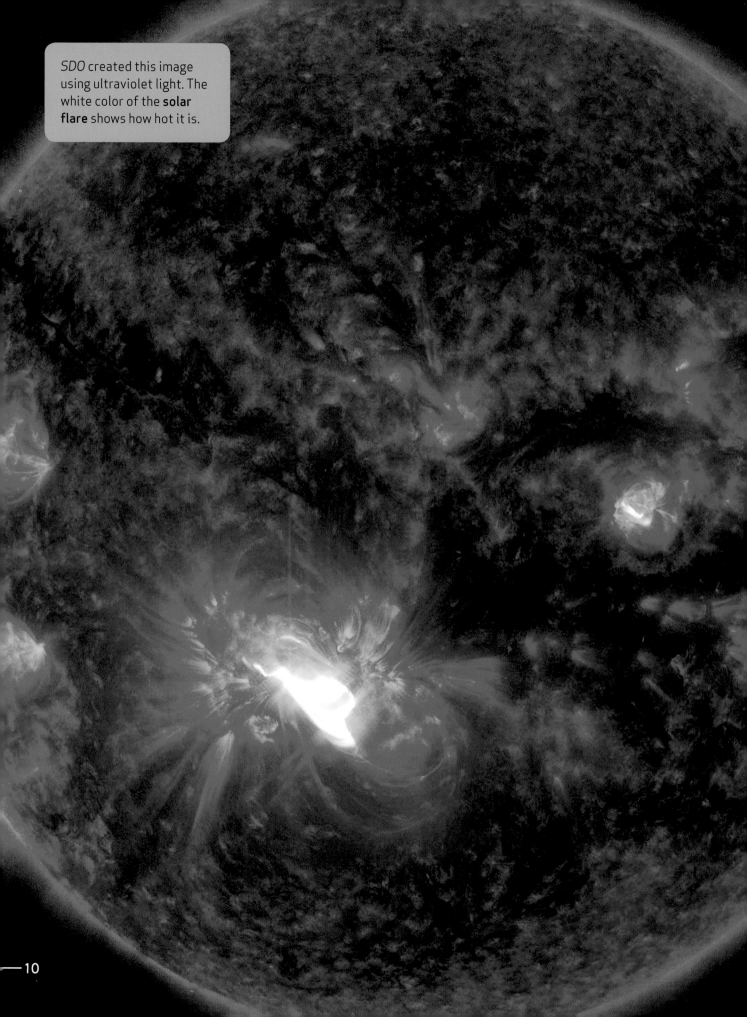

SDO created this image using ultraviolet light. The white color of the **solar flare** shows how hot it is.

THE SUN:
A WOW DISCOVERY

In October 2014, the Sun's surface was very active—there were more sunspots than usual. *SDO* was able to take amazing photographs!

Enormous eruptions

On October 18, astronomers noticed one of the biggest sunspots ever seen. It was about the size of Jupiter! Sunspots look darker because they are cooler than the surrounding area. This massive sunspot released six huge and four small explosions of energy called solar flares.

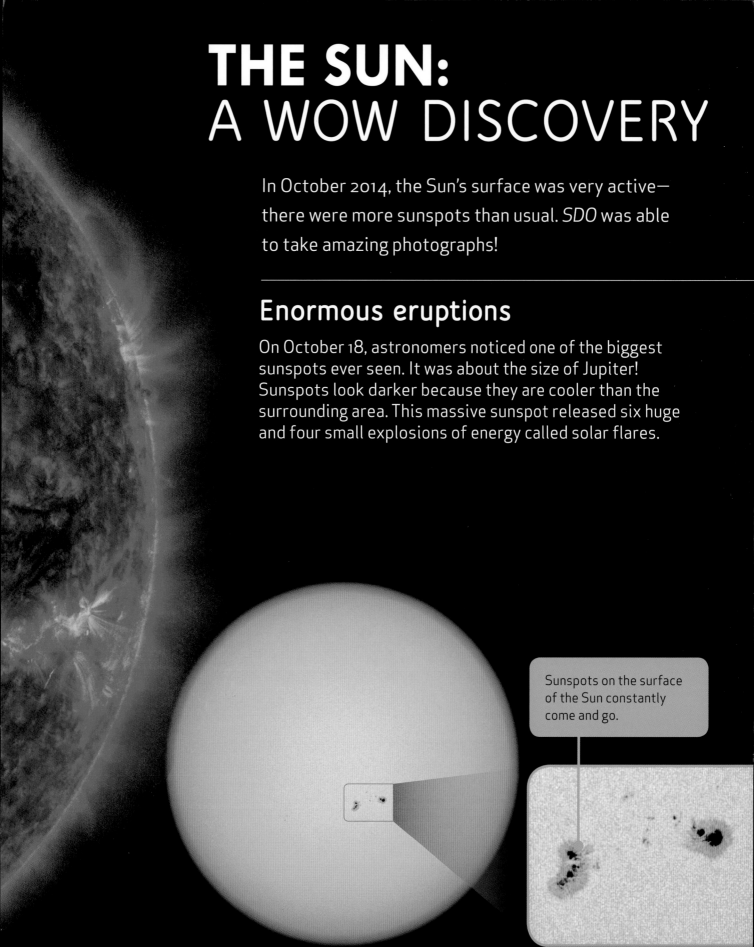

Sunspots on the surface of the Sun constantly come and go.

LITTLE MERCURY

The closest planet to the Sun—Mercury—is also the smallest.
Mercury is a small ball of rock, with a surface marked by **craters**.
The temperature there swings from sizzling hot to freezing cold.

Speedy messenger

Mercury is named after the Roman messenger god who wore
winged sandals to speed through the air. The planet travels
through space faster than any other, making a complete
orbit of the Sun every 88 days. The only thing it does slowly
is spin—a day on Mercury lasts for 59 Earth days.

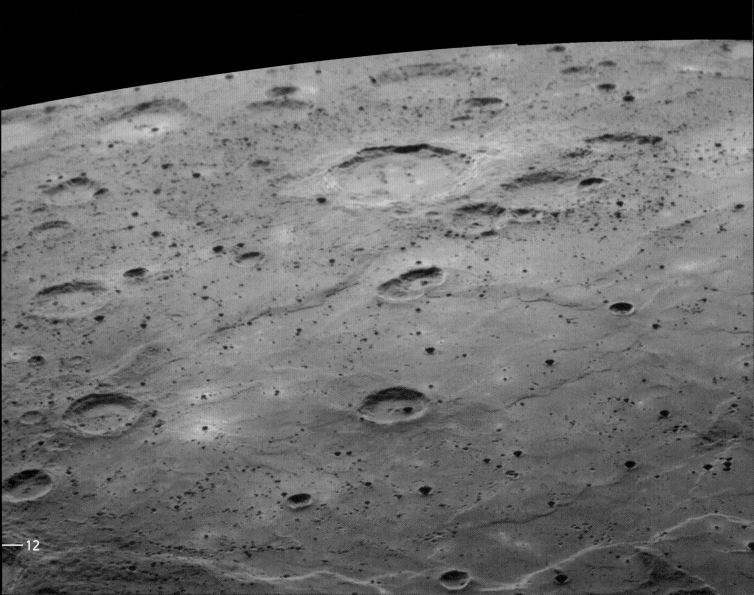

Observing Mercury

Mercury is so close to the Sun that it is difficult to see. The best times to spot the planet in the sky are at dawn or dusk. Astronomers can sometimes see Mercury as a black dot traveling across the surface of the Sun. This is called a transit, and it happens 13 times each century.

Fake neighbor

In 1859, a French mathematician suggested there might be another planet between Mercury and the Sun. He thought this would explain the mysterious wobbles in Mercury's orbit. He called this new planet Vulcan, and astronomers around the world soon claimed to have spotted it. But it never existed!

Mercury's cratered surface looks a bit like Earth's moon.

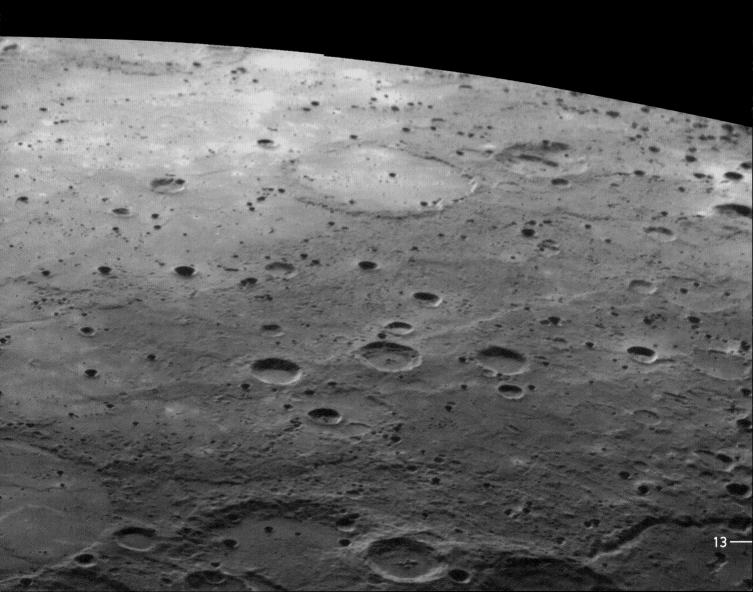

MERCURY:
A MISSION REPORT

960 MILES

THE WIDTH OF MERCURY'S LARGEST CRATER

The spacecraft

Messenger was launched on August 3, 2004. It reached Mercury almost four years later. After flying close to Mercury a couple of times, *Messenger* went into orbit around the planet in March 2011. At the end of its mission, on April 30, 2015, *Messenger* was deliberately crashed into the planet's surface. It is estimated the impact created a 52-foot-wide crater.

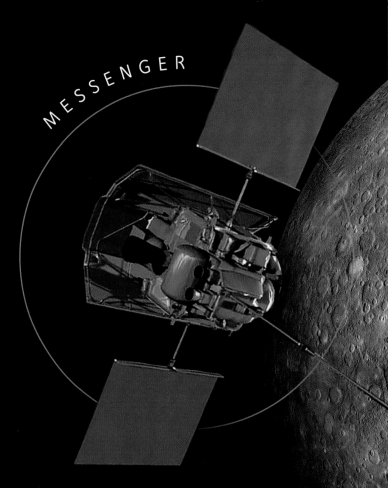

MESSENGER

29 MILLION MILES

MERCURY'S CLOSEST POSITION TO THE SUN

Can we live there?

Mercury is too close to the Sun to support life. Its **magnetic field** provides some protection from the Sun's harmful **radiation**. However, *Messenger* discovered the magnetic field is "leaky," allowing some radiation through.

What's the weather like?

Mercury has a thin **atmosphere**. It is close to the Sun, so there are no storms, clouds, winds, or rain. It gets scorching hot during the day, with temperatures of up to 801 °F. But it also becomes freezing cold at night, dropping to -290 °F!

When large rocks hit Mercury, they kick up smaller rocks from the surface. When the smaller rocks land again, they cause even more craters.

What does Mercury look like?

The craters on Mercury's surface were made when large space rocks crashed into the planet millions of years ago. *Messenger* provided the first proof that there are volcanoes on Mercury, although they are no longer active.

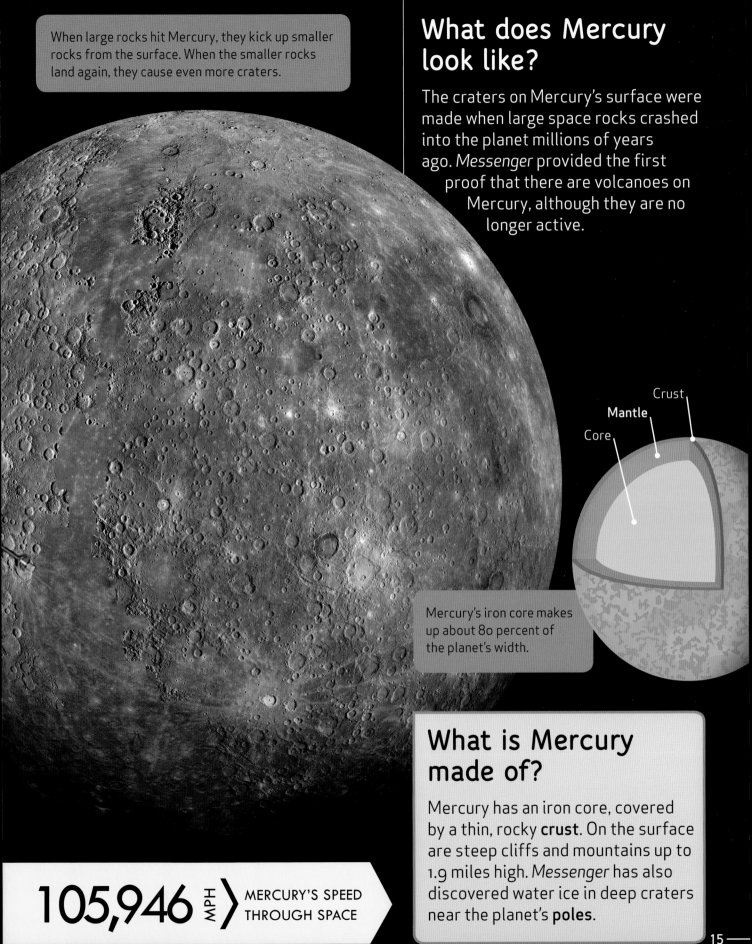

Crust

Mantle

Core

Mercury's iron core makes up about 80 percent of the planet's width.

What is Mercury made of?

Mercury has an iron core, covered by a thin, rocky **crust**. On the surface are steep cliffs and mountains up to 1.9 miles high. *Messenger* has also discovered water ice in deep craters near the planet's **poles**.

105,946 MPH ⟩ MERCURY'S SPEED THROUGH SPACE

MERCURY:
A WOW DISCOVERY

Some craters near Mercury's poles are always in shadow. Although the temperatures elsewhere on the planet are high, these craters stay cold enough to contain ice.

Hidden ice

Messenger took the first photos inside the icy craters. Because no sunlight reaches deep inside, the temperature stays low. In some craters that are slightly farther from the poles, there is also water ice. Astronomers think the water may originally have come from comets smashing into Mercury long ago.

In this image, hot areas are colored red and cold areas are purple. The coldest areas are deep inside Mercury's craters.

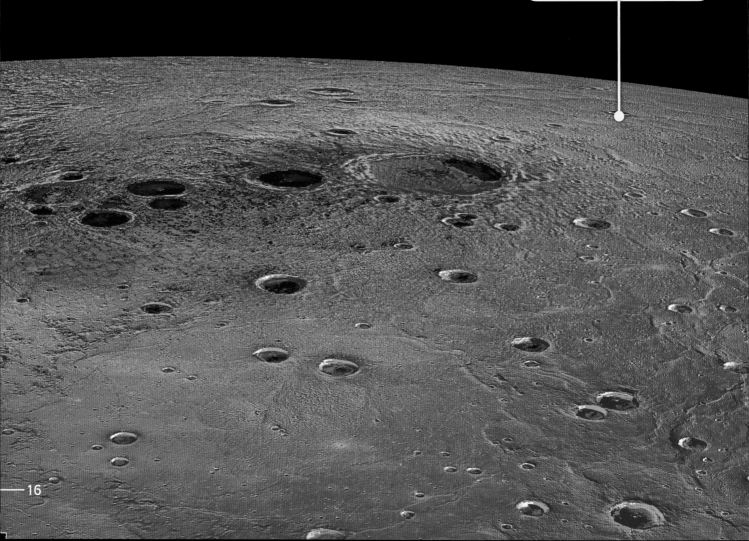

HOT VENUS

Venus was named after the Roman goddess of beauty, but with blistering temperatures and toxic gases, it's somewhere that no one would want to visit!

Bright in the sky

After the Sun and the Moon, Venus is the brightest object in the night sky and can be seen just as the Sun is rising or setting. It is often called "the morning star" or "the evening star." The clouds that surround Venus reflect the Sun's light, but they also block our view. We have only been able to get our first glimpses of its surface with **radar** imaging—using radio waves to detect objects.

Photographs of Venus only show the clouds surrounding the planet.

VENUS:
A MISSION REPORT

The spacecraft

In 1989, *Magellan* was launched from the space shuttle—a reusable space plane. It was able to create detailed images of Venus' rocky surface. In 2005, a robotic probe called *Venus Express* was launched. It studied the planet's atmosphere and weather. After finishing their missions, both spacecraft sank into the clouds and were destroyed.

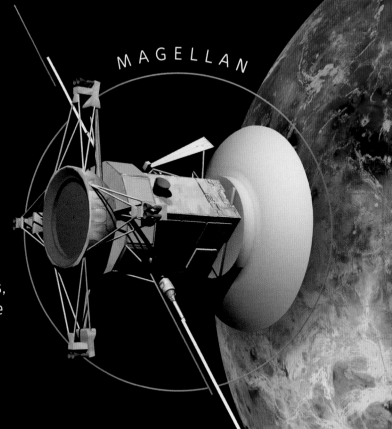

MAGELLAN

Is Venus like Earth?

Venus is slightly smaller than Earth. Both planets have a metal core, a mantle of hot rock, and a crust of solid rock. Earth's atmosphere supports life, but Venus' is much thicker and is mostly made up of **carbon dioxide**. This traps the Sun's heat, making Venus incredibly hot. It's like the greenhouse effect on Earth, only much more powerful.

Crust

Mantle

Core

What's on the surface?

Magellan's radar let astronomers "see" through the clouds to study the surface of Venus. The planet has no oceans, but there are mountains, craters, and plains. Two "continents" of higher land stand out from the rest.

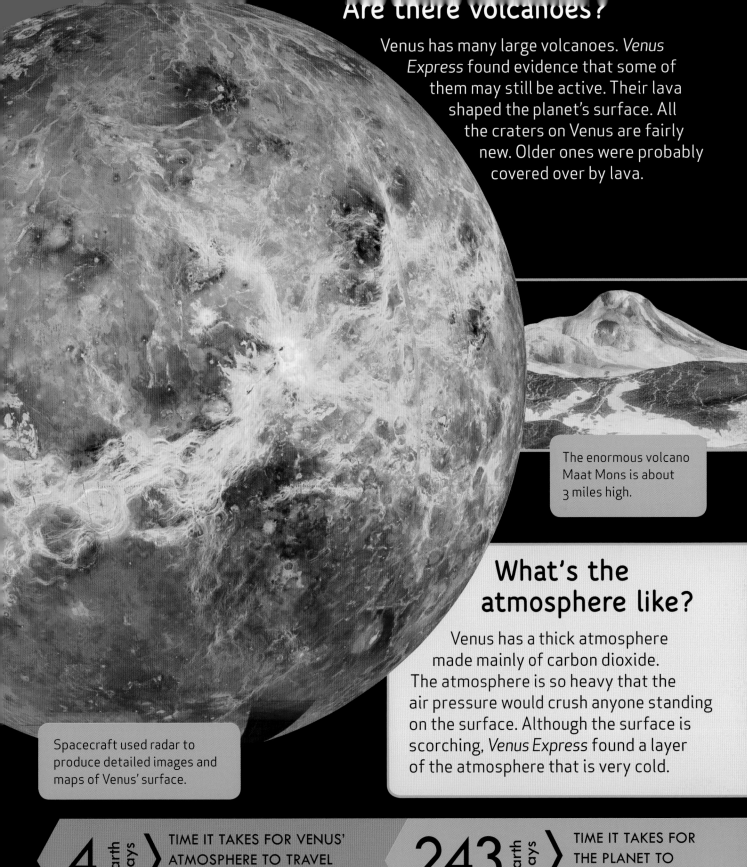

Are there volcanoes?

Venus has many large volcanoes. *Venus Express* found evidence that some of them may still be active. Their lava shaped the planet's surface. All the craters on Venus are fairly new. Older ones were probably covered over by lava.

The enormous volcano Maat Mons is about 3 miles high.

What's the atmosphere like?

Venus has a thick atmosphere made mainly of carbon dioxide. The atmosphere is so heavy that the air pressure would crush anyone standing on the surface. Although the surface is scorching, *Venus Express* found a layer of the atmosphere that is very cold.

Spacecraft used radar to produce detailed images and maps of Venus' surface.

4 Earth days › TIME IT TAKES FOR VENUS' ATMOSPHERE TO TRAVEL ONCE AROUND THE PLANET

243 Earth days › TIME IT TAKES FOR THE PLANET TO ROTATE ONCE

VENUS:
A WOW DISCOVERY

When *Venus Express* measured the hydrogen in the planet's atmosphere, it showed the planet once contained a lot of water—and possibly oceans on the surface.

Where did the water go?

There is a tiny amount of water vapor in Venus' clouds, but it is disappearing. *Venus Express* found water molecules split up into hydrogen and oxygen atoms in the planet's atmosphere. Then, **solar wind**—a stream of particles from the Sun—carries these atoms into space. *Venus Express* also discovered the planet's atmosphere is so cold in some places that it makes carbon dioxide snow!

Venus Express discovered that Venus produces electricity, which removes oxygen from the atmosphere.

OUR EARTH

Earth is the third planet from the Sun, and the largest of the four rocky planets. Its oceans and atmosphere make it the perfect place for life to flourish.

Inside Earth

Like the other rocky planets, Earth is made of different layers. At the center is a core of solid metal, which is surrounded by a layer of super-hot molten (liquid) metal. Outside that layer is the mantle, a layer of hot, soft rock. We live on the crust, which is a thin, hard layer. The continents are part of the crust, and the oceans fill the crust's lower areas.

There is so much water on Earth that it looks blue from space.

The spacecraft

There are more than 1,000 artificial **satellites** in orbit around Earth. Some transmit television and phone signals; others provide data for GPS receivers. NASA's *Earth Observing System* (*EOS*) is a group of satellites powered by solar panels, which capture the Sun's rays and convert them into electricity.

92 minutes

THE TIME IT TAKES FOR THE INTERNATIONAL SPACE STATION TO GO AROUND EARTH ONCE

Mapping Earth

The Landsat satellites have pr
images of Earth's surface for o
40 years. They go around Earth
than 14 times a day, and take 16
to scan the surface of the entir
planet. Their images are used b
scientists, as well as for online

Lan
like
Los
a bi
of t

What's the atmosphere like?

Earth has an atmosphere of gases that surrounds the planet like a blanket. The movement of air in the atmosphere causes wind and weather. An *EOS* satellite called *Terra* measures temperature and clouds, and monitors air pollution. It studies how human activity is changing the climate.

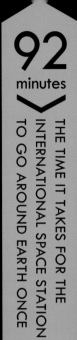

Atmosphere

Some satellites orbit high up in the atmosphere, while some are much lower.

134°F

TEMPERATURE

HIGHEST TEMPERATURE EVER RECORDED ON EARTH, ON JULY 10, 1913, IN DEATH VALLEY, CALIFORNIA

How do astronauts study Earth?

Astronauts work and live for 6 months at a time on a giant artificial satellite called the International Space Station. One of their main jobs is to study how weightlessness affects the human body, plants, and materials. They also look at Earth and its weather.

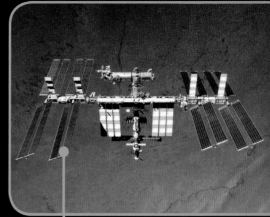

The International Space Station has large solar panels that provide electricity.

TERRA

447 MILES ❯ HEIGHT OF TERRA SATELLITE ABOVE EARTH

How has Earth changed?

Satellites that study Earth have observed big changes over the years. Their images show where land has been changed by fire, floods, volcanoes, or cutting down forests. They track the movement of **glaciers**, and the growing and shrinking of the polar ice caps. They also follow huge storms as they swirl around the planet.

Looking at nighttime lights shows how densely populated some cities are, and how empty other land areas are.

EARTH:
A WOW DISCOVERY

Astronauts traveling to the Moon took the first clear photos showing our entire planet. Since then, satellites and spacecraft have given us even more amazing images.

Black marble

The *Suomi NPP* is an advanced weather satellite that travels around Earth. Scientists used data they collected over several days to create this "black marble" image of Earth at night. It took 312 complete orbits for the satellite to get a clear shot of every part of Earth. The land is covered in a spiderweb of lights—showing that the electric lights of our towns and cities are visible from space!

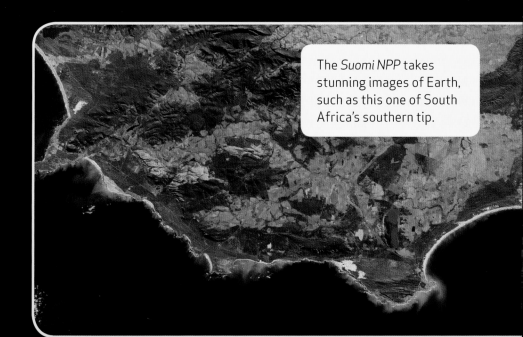

The *Suomi NPP* takes stunning images of Earth, such as this one of South Africa's southern tip.

EARTH'S MOON

Aside from the Sun, the Moon is the brightest object in the night sky. Its pale surface reflects the Sun's rays, lighting up our nights—and sometimes the days too!

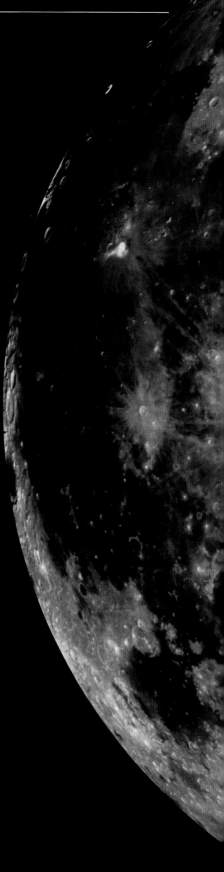

Constant companion

It takes about 28 days for the Moon to complete one orbit of Earth. During this time, the Moon appears to shrink from a disk to a tiny crescent, then grows full again. This happens because as the Moon orbits Earth, the amount of the lit side we see changes.

Feeling the pull

The Moon is fairly small, but it is close enough that its gravity has an effect on Earth. The Moon's gravity pulls at the water in Earth's oceans, making it bulge out. These bulges create the high tides at the coasts twice a day.

The perfect size

The Moon orbits Earth at an average distance of 238,855 miles. This seems like a long way, but the Sun is 400 times farther away. It is also 400 times bigger than the Moon, making the two objects appear about the same size in the sky. This match-up makes it possible for us to view amazing total **eclipses** of the Sun.

The Moon's landscape is a mix of low, dark plains and bright areas of higher land.

THE MOON:
A MISSION REPORT

12

THE NUMBER OF PEOPLE WHO HAVE WALKED ON THE MOON

The spacecraft

From 1969 to 1972, 12 astronauts visited the Moon. In 1994, NASA's *Clementine* entered orbit around the Moon and took detailed photos of its entire surface. In 2009, *Lunar Reconnaissance Orbiter* (*LRO*) arrived at the Moon. It used advanced tools to create a 3D map of the Moon's surface. It was looking for safe landing sites for future missions.

Could we live there?

The Moon is the only place beyond Earth that astronauts have visited. None of them stayed on the surface for more than a few days. To live there for longer, we would need sources of water and oxygen, as well as protection from radiation and extreme temperatures.

What's the Moon made of?

Many scientists believe that billions of years ago, a large object crashed into Earth, breaking off pieces of rock and dust. Some of these pieces clumped together to form the Moon.

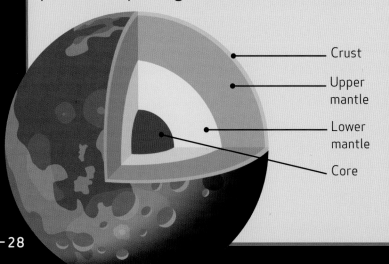

- Crust
- Upper mantle
- Lower mantle
- Core

1.6
MILLION

THE NUMBER OF PHOTOS TAKEN BY CLEMENTINE

Why are there so many craters?

Spacecraft have mapped thousands of craters on the Moon's surface. They were caused by asteroids and other objects crashing into it. With no lava to cover them, and no wind or rain to wash them away, the craters have lasted for billions of years.

Astronauts took this photo of a crater in 1972. You can see their vehicle parked in the background.

LRO

What's the weather like?

The Moon has an extremely thin atmosphere. It cannot protect the Moon from the Sun's radiation. During the day, the temperature soars to 260 °F, but at night it drops to −280 °F. India's *Chandrayaan-1* spacecraft arrived at the Moon in 2008. It detected small amounts of water vapour in the exosphere.

THE MOON:
A WOW DISCOVERY

To live on the Moon, astronauts would need water. A recent mission by the *LCROSS* spacecraft showed that water might already be there in the form of ice.

Impact!

LCROSS was a separate spacecraft that launched with *LRO* in 2009. Its job was to cause an impact at the Moon's pole to test for water ice. After separating, *LCROSS* carried part of its booster rocket closer to the Moon and then let go, sending it crashing into the Moon. The launch vehicle landed in a crater near the south pole, which is in permanent shadow. *LCROSS* followed, using its tools to analyze the dust thrown up by the impact. It found that there are large amounts of water ice on the Moon.

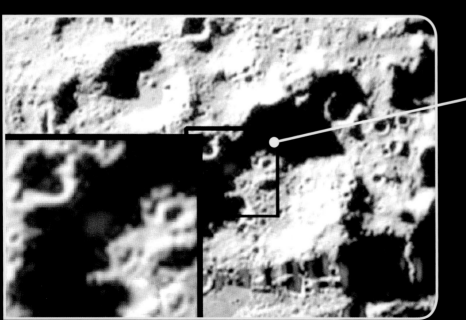

LCROSS discovered about 26 gallons of water in this crater.

After studying the dust from the impact, *LCROSS* was crashed into the Moon's surface.

PHOBOS

Mars' two moons, Phobos and Deimos, were discovered in 1877 by American astronomer Asaph Hall.

THE RED PLANET

The fourth planet from the Sun, Mars is small and rocky. It may once have been more like Earth—and may even have supported life.

Color of rust

Mars' red color can be seen from Earth. Because red is the color of blood, the planet was named after the Roman god of war. Other cultures noticed its color, too. The ancient Egyptians called it "Horus the Red," after one of their important gods. In China it was known as the "fire star." We now know that the red color is caused by iron oxide (rust) on the planet's surface.

DEIMOS

Tiny moons

Mars has two moons, Deimos and Phobos, named after horses belonging to Ares, the Greek god of war. Our Moon is about one-quarter as wide as Earth, but Mars' moons are tiny in comparison. Phobos is about 16 miles wide, and Deimos is even smaller. Scientists think they are asteroids that were captured by the planet's gravity.

Martian canals

In 1877, Italian astronomer Giovanni Schiaparelli drew maps of the surface of Mars. He saw long, straight lines, which he marked as "canali." This means "channels" in Italian, but it was translated into English as "canals." Some people thought this meant that living things had dug canals on the surface, leading to stories about Martians. We now know these were naturally formed surface features.

MARS:
A MISSION REPORT

The spacecraft

MAVEN entered orbit around Mars in 2014. It studies the planet's atmosphere and looks at the effects of the solar wind—a stream of particles from the Sun. The *Curiosity* **rover** landed on the surface in 2012 and has since traveled more than 10.5 miles. It has cameras, drills, and tools for analyzing rock samples. It is looking for signs of water and life.

MAVEN

37.5 POUNDS

WHAT 100 POUNDS WEIGHS ON MARS

What's at the poles?

Like Earth, Mars has ice caps at its north and south poles. However, Earth's ice caps are made of water ice; whereas the ice caps on Mars are a mixture of water and frozen carbon dioxide. The *Mars Reconnaissance Orbiter* showed that Mars had ice ages in the past, like Earth.

What's the weather like?

Mars has a thin atmosphere that is mostly made up of carbon dioxide. *MAVEN* showed the atmosphere used to be thicker, but the solar wind stripped much of it away. The atmosphere is now too thin to trap the Sun's heat. Although the temperature can reach 70 °F on a summer day, at night it plunges to −100 °F.

What's on the surface?

As it drives across the surface, *Curiosity* has avoided craters and deep canyons. There are also volcanoes, though they are no longer active. Red dust covers most of the planet's surface. Strong winds blow the dust around in huge storms.

The canyon Valles Marineris is about as long as the United States is wide.

Is there life on Mars?

Scientists have searched for signs of life on Mars. If there were ever life forms on Mars, it would likely have been microbes such as **bacteria**. In 2016, scientists found large amounts of underground water, which living things would need. However, in 2017 they discovered the surface of Mars contains a chemical that is toxic to bacteria.

Curiosity sent back this "selfie" taken on the surface of Mars.

24.62 HOURS
THE LENGTH OF A DAY ON MARS

MARS:
A WOW DISCOVERY

Astronomers have known for a while that there is frozen water on Mars. Recently they discovered proof that water once flowed as a liquid across the planet's surface.

Based on the size of the stones, astronomers think this stream was once between ankle-deep and hip-deep.

Water world

In 2012, the *Curiosity* rover took a photo of a rock formation that contained an important clue. It showed gravel that included some smoothly rounded stones. This is a sign they were once carried by flowing water, like the smooth stones in a stream on Earth.

The largest pebbles in *Curiosity*'s photo were about the size of golf balls.

INTO THE ASTEROIDS

Beyond Mars, there is a huge gap before you reach the next planet. But this space isn't empty—it is home to millions of smaller objects called asteroids.

Mini marvels

Asteroids are rocky and very small. If all the asteroids were combined together, they would still make an object smaller than Earth's Moon. Asteroids also come in many different shapes, because they don't have enough **mass** for their gravity to pull them into a ball shape.

Looking for a planet

At the end of the 18th century, some astronomers began to look for a planet they believed was orbiting between Mars and Jupiter. After Italian astronomer Giuseppe Piazzi discovered the space object Ceres in 1801, and then more small objects were discovered in that area, they realized that the objects were not planets, but asteroids.

Headed for Earth?

Most asteroids orbit the Sun in a wide "belt" between Mars and Jupiter. However, the gravity of larger objects can easily throw them off course, sending them hurtling through the Solar System. Astronomers keep a close eye on asteroids with paths that may cross Earth's orbit.

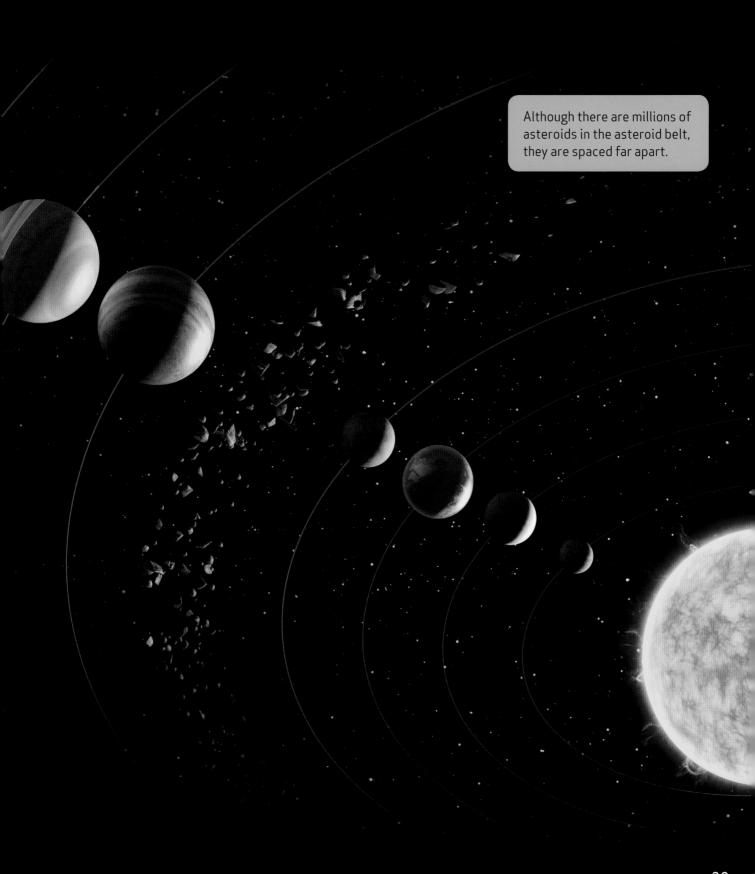

Although there are millions of asteroids in the asteroid belt, they are spaced far apart.

ASTEROIDS:
A MISSION REPORT

363 YEARS

THE TIME IT TAKES FOR VESTA TO TRAVEL AROUND THE SUN

The spacecraft

In 2000, the *NEAR Shoemaker* probe became the first spacecraft to orbit an asteroid. The following year, it landed on the asteroid's surface and sent back information. The *Dawn* probe launched in 2007. It spent over a year orbiting and mapping Vesta, the largest asteroid, before moving on to study a **dwarf planet**.

What are asteroids like?

Asteroids are not all the same—they fall into three main categories. The most common are made of rock. Some asteroids are made of metals such as nickel and iron. Others are a mixture of rock and metals. *NEAR Shoemaker* discovered Eros is the same all the way through. It does not have a core, mantle, and crust.

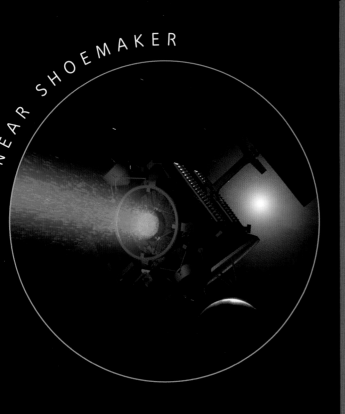

NEAR SHOEMAKER

330 MILES

WIDTH OF VESTA, THE LARGEST ASTEROID

Can asteroids have moons?

In 1993, *Galileo* discovered a tiny moon orbiting the asteroid Ida. Since then, astronomers have found several hundred more asteroids with moons.

Where are asteroids found?

1.9 MILLION ⟩ ESTIMATED NUMBER OF ASTEROIDS IN THE ASTEROID BELT

Many asteroids are in the "belt" between Mars and Jupiter. Others, called trojans, share the orbit of a planet. They travel in two groups—one ahead of the planet, and one behind. Jupiter has a huge number of trojans. Some near-Earth asteroids orbit just outside or just inside our planet's path. Astronomers use telescopes on the ground to spot near-Earth asteroids.

Eros is about 20 miles long and covered with craters.

Many scientists believe that an asteroid crashing into Earth killed the dinosaurs.

Where did they come from?

Asteroids are the leftovers from the formation of the Solar System. Large asteroids crashed into each other, eventually clumping together to form planets. By studying asteroids, astronomers can learn more about what the early Solar System was like.

VESTA:
A WOW DISCOVERY

Asteroids are too small and too far away to see clearly from Earth, even with a powerful telescope. *Dawn* sent back the first clear images of Vesta in 2011.

Close encounter

Dawn had a powerful camera, as well as tools for studying Vesta's gravity and makeup. During its time orbiting the asteroid, *Dawn* came as close as 130 miles from the surface. It found hundreds of craters, from enormous to tiny. It also discovered a mountain near Vesta's south pole that is twice as tall as Mount Everest.

Vesta is almost **spherical** in shape.

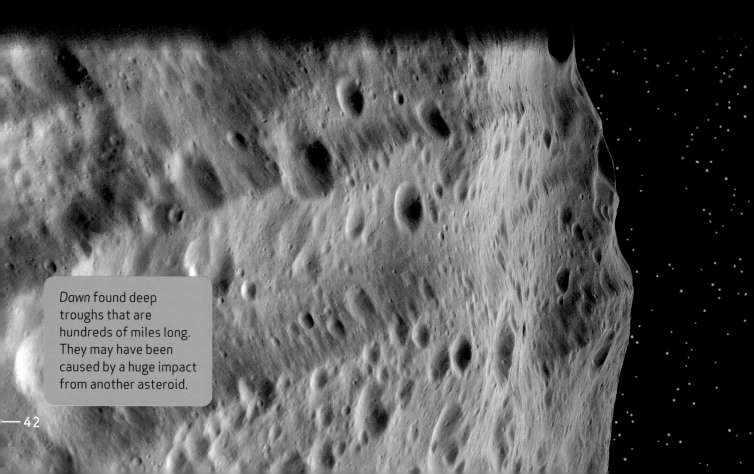

Dawn found deep troughs that are hundreds of miles long. They may have been caused by a huge impact from another asteroid.

KING JUPITER

Past the asteroid belt is Jupiter—a giant gas planet that is almost 2.5 times more massive than all the other planets combined.

Giant of the Solar System

Jupiter is named after the king of the Roman gods and is one of the brightest objects in the night sky. In 1610, Italian astronomer Galileo Galilei spotted four small objects near Jupiter. He had just discovered the first moons orbiting another planet. The largest of them, Ganymede, is even bigger than Mercury. Since then, astronomers have found more than 60 smaller moons orbiting Jupiter.

IO

EUROPA

GANYMEDE

CALISTO

Jupiter's four largest moons are called the "Galilean moons" in honor of their discoverer.

JUPITER:
A MISSION REPORT

9.9 HOURS

TIME IT TAKES FOR JUPITER TO ROTATE ONCE

The spacecraft

Galileo launched in 1989 and took six years to reach Jupiter. It became the first spacecraft to orbit Jupiter, and it launched a probe into the planet's atmosphere. A second **orbiter**, *Juno*, was launched in 2011. Arriving in 2016, it soon began sending back data as well as amazing photos.

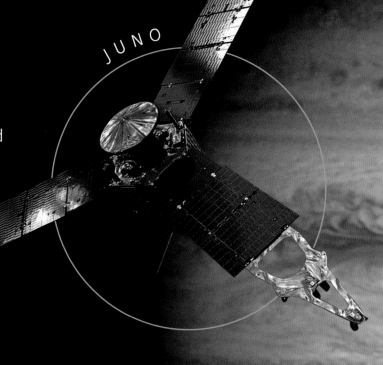

JUNO

What does Jupiter look like?

Jupiter's surface is covered by clouds, which are constantly on the move. In 1994, *Galileo* recorded 21 pieces of a comet smashing into Jupiter. They left temporary dark "scars" on the planet's surface.

-234°F

AVERAGE TEMPERATURE ON JUPITER

What is Jupiter made of?

One of *Juno*'s missions is to learn more about what's inside Jupiter. The "surface" we see is made up of swirling clouds. Jupiter is mainly made of hydrogen and helium gas—the same gases that form the Sun. Astronomers are hoping that *Juno* will discover whether there is a solid core deep inside.

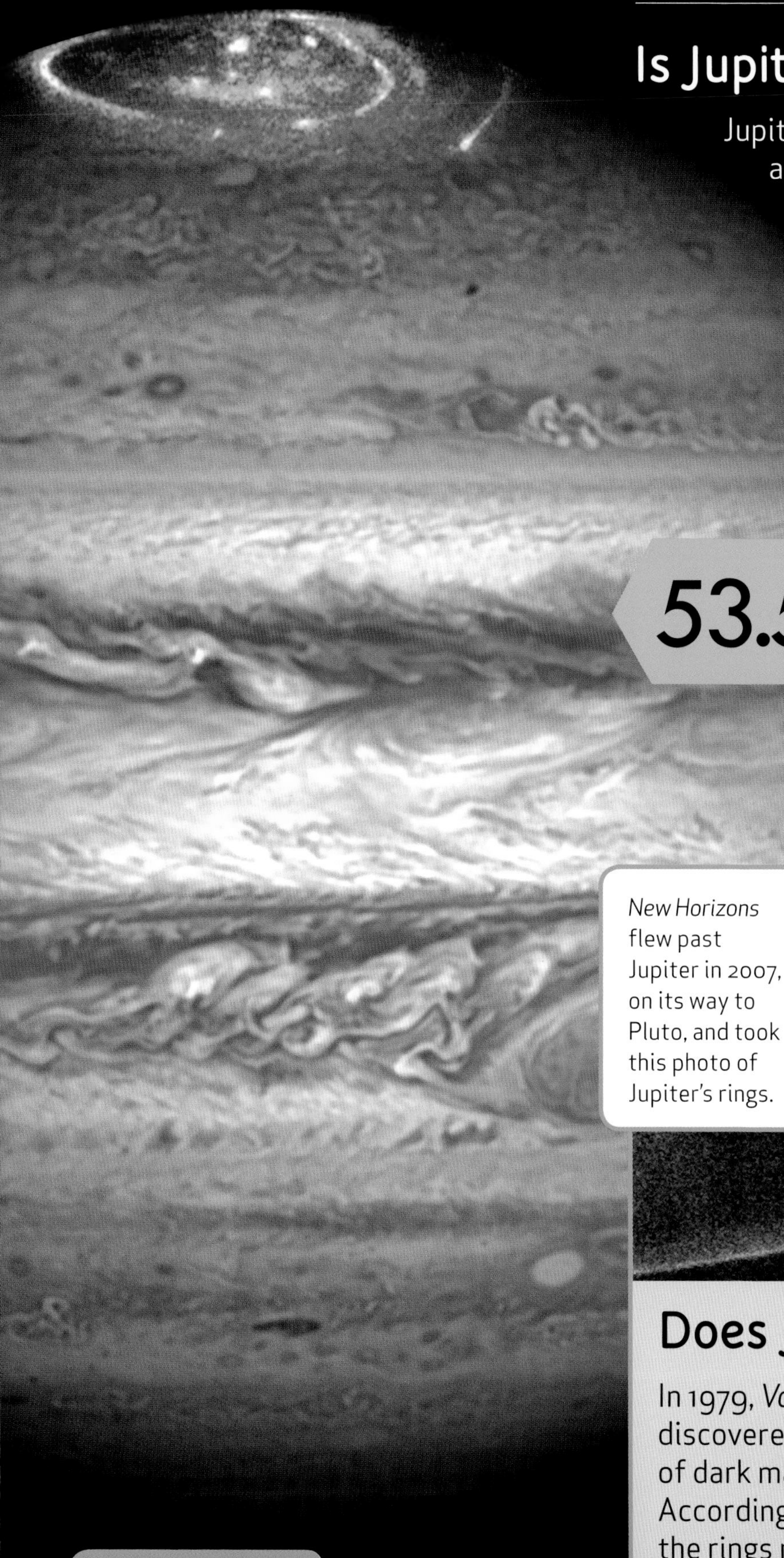

Is Jupiter magnetic?

Jupiter has a powerful magnetic field—
an area of magnetic force— that
extends far out into space. It may
be caused by the planet's fast
rotation. Near the planet,
the magnetic field creates
radiation that can
damage spacecraft.

53.5 HOURS > TIME IT TAKES FOR JUNO
TO COMPLETE ONE
ORBIT OF JUPITER

New Horizons
flew past
Jupiter in 2007,
on its way to
Pluto, and took
this photo of
Jupiter's rings.

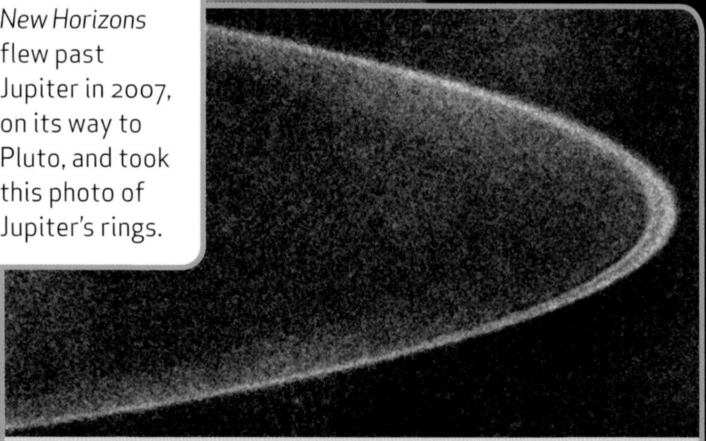

Does Jupiter have rings?

In 1979, *Voyager* flew past Jupiter and
discovered three rings. They are made
of dark material that is difficult to see.
According to data sent back by *Galileo*,
the rings might be made of dust kicked up
when objects crashed into Jupiter's moons.

Jupiter has amazing
light shows called
auroras at its poles.

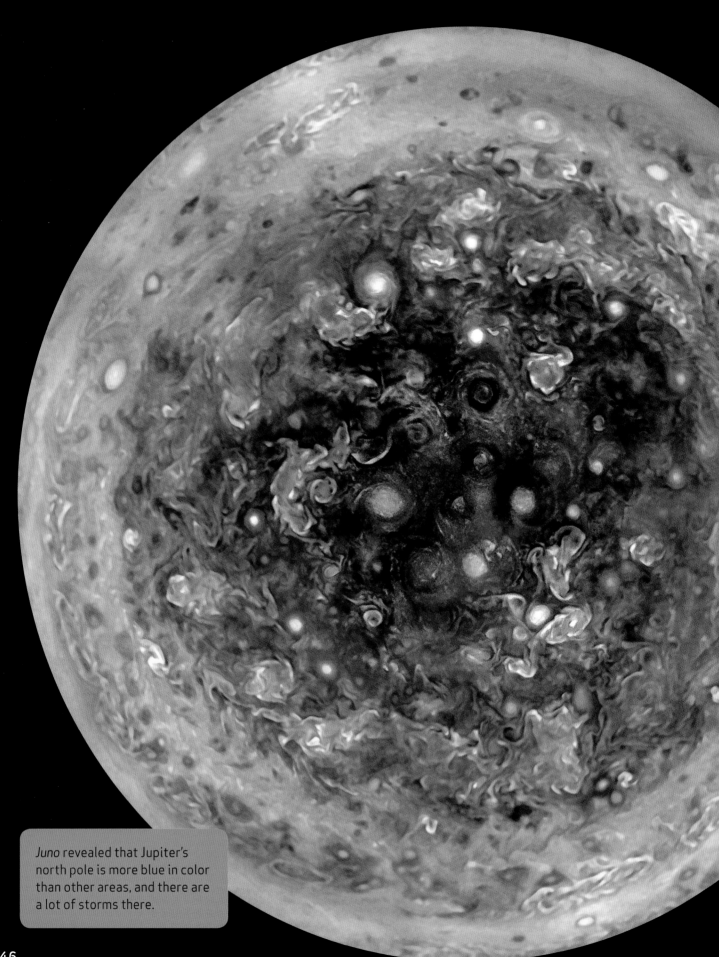

Juno revealed that Jupiter's north pole is more blue in color than other areas, and there are a lot of storms there.

JUPITER:
A WOW DISCOVERY

Astronomers have known about Jupiter's swirling storms for decades. However, amazing new photographs from the *Juno* mission let us see the clouds as never before.

Colored clouds

Although most of the planet is made up of hydrogen and helium gas, the clouds are made of ammonia crystals. Powerful storms bring other chemicals, such as phosphorus and sulfur, into contact with the clouds. Ammonia reacts with these chemicals, creating dazzling bands of color. *Juno* discovered the clouds swirl in patterns rather than being arranged in stripes. It also gave our first views of the poles.

Jupiter's Great Red Spot is an Earth-sized storm that has raged for hundreds of years.

MAGNIFICENT SATURN

Saturn can be instantly recognized by its beautiful rings. Scientists are only now unraveling some of the mysteries of the planet, its rings, and its moons.

Clear rings

In 1610, Galileo observed Saturn through his telescope, but it wasn't powerful enough to show the rings clearly. Instead, Galileo thought he was seeing a planet with a moon on each side. Nearly 50 years later, Christiaan Huygens used a much more powerful telescope and realized the planet actually had rings around it.

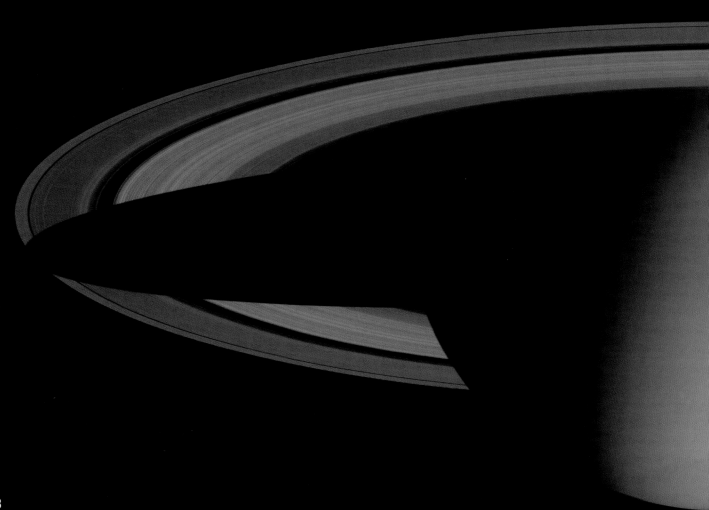

The Saturn system

Saturn is surrounded by at least 60 moons, including one that is larger than Mercury. Some of the moons orbit within the rings, while others are much farther out. Inside the rings there are also many smaller "moonlets" just a few hundred feet wide. These moonlets make faint streaks in the rings, which can be seen by orbiting spacecraft.

Floating planet

At the center of Saturn is a solid core of rock, ice, and other materials, surrounded by a layer of liquid and then a layer of gas. Like Jupiter, Saturn is made mostly of hydrogen and helium gas. These light gases mean that the planet is not very dense. In fact, it would float if it were placed in water!

Cassini took this magnificent photo of Saturn before going into orbit around the planet.

SATURN:
A MISSION REPORT

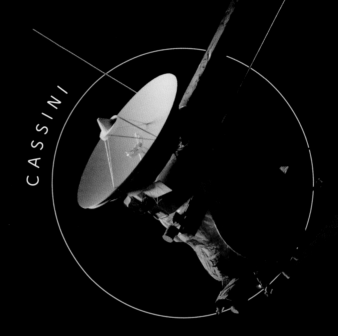

The spacecraft

Cassini launched in 1997 and began its orbit of Saturn in 2004. It sent back information about the planet's atmosphere, magnetic field, and rings. It carried out **flybys** of many of Saturn's moons, and it even sent a **lander** down to the surface of the largest moon, Titan.

1,600 FEET PER SECOND
SPEED OF WINDS IN THE UPPER ATMOSPHERE

What's the weather like?

Saturn has powerful storms with winds five times faster than the biggest storms on Earth. The gases in the atmosphere create air pressure so strong that it can force gas into a liquid state. Any spacecraft entering the atmosphere would be crushed. This is what happened to *Cassini* when its mission finished.

-288°F
AVERAGE TEMPERATURE ON SATURN

Cassini saw a storm that was more than 11,000 miles long.

How old are Saturn's rings?

Astronomers once thought that the rings were formed from the remains of a comet smashing into a moon. However, *Cassini* has shown that different rings were created at different times, and that the materials in the rings are constantly being recycled. They may be billions of years old.

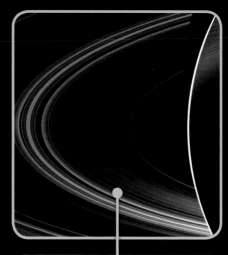

Saturn's rings are divided into seven main bands.

What are the moons like?

Saturn has some very unusual moons. One of Saturn's moons, Iapetus, is black on one side and white on the other. *Cassini* may have discovered why. During Iapetus' long days, the dark material takes in heat from the Sun and warms up. Any ice turns to gas and refreezes in the colder regions. This makes the dark side darker and the light side lighter.

A WOW DISCOVERY

Saturn is a very stormy planet. Scientists have flown *Cassini* dangerously close to the planet's surface to take incredible pictures of hurricanes and storms.

A six-sided storm

One of the most amazing discoveries by *Cassini* has been a huge, powerful hexagon-shaped storm around the planet's north pole. The storm is 18,640 miles across, which means you could fit two Earths inside it! The winds in the storm are swirling around at speeds of 200 miles per hour.

Scientists think this storm has been raging on Saturn for at least 30 years.

TREMENDOUS TITAN

Saturn's largest moon is an odd place. It is a bit like Earth, but with some very important differences. Thanks to *Cassini*, we now know a lot about it.

What's in a name?

Titan was the first of Saturn's moons to be discovered, by Christiaan Huygens in 1655. Saturn was named after a Roman god, and the Greek version of that god was called Cronus. In Greek mythology, Cronus belonged to the Titans, a group of giant gods. This is where the moon gets its name. Some of Saturn's other moons—including Rhea, Phoebe, and Hyperion—are named after other Titans. Others are named after giants in the myths and legends of other cultures.

After Ganymede, Titan is the largest moon in the Solar System.

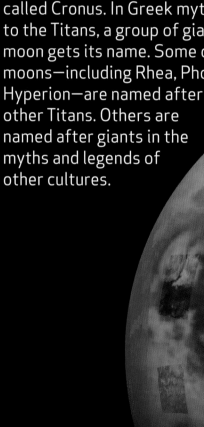

TITAN:
A MISSION REPORT

The spacecraft

On December 25, 2004, *Cassini* released a small lander called *Huygens*, which then parachuted to the surface of Titan. For 90 minutes, it sent data to Earth. *Huygens* carried tools for measuring materials in the atmosphere as well as the wind speed.

What's below the clouds?

Titan is the only moon with a thick atmosphere. From a distance, it looks like a fuzzy orange ball. These clouds hide a large, rocky moon that makes a complete trip around Saturn about once every 16 days.

Huygens was nearly 9 feet in diameter and weighed 705 pounds.

Huygens snapped this photo of Titan's frozen surface on its way down.

3,200 MILES ❯ THE WIDTH OF TITAN, MAKING IT BIGGER THAN MERCURY

What's the weather like?

Titan's atmosphere is mostly made up of nitrogen gas and **methane**. The air pressure is so high that standing on Titan would feel like standing at the bottom of a swimming pool. Like Saturn, the moon is also very cold at about −290 °F.

Could we live there?

Titan has a solid surface and an atmosphere, but it's not the kind of air we can breathe. Astronauts would need an oxygen mask and protection from the incredibly cold temperatures. There is little risk of radiation, and the gravity is so weak that astronauts could fly by wearing wings.

525 FEET

DEEPEST POINT OF LIGEIA MARE, ONE OF TITAN'S SEAS

5%

THE PERCENTAGE OF METHANE IN TITAN'S ATMOSPHERE

Where does the methane come from?

On Earth, methane is a gas. On Titan, it is so cold that methane turns into a liquid that falls from the sky and flows across the surface. Sunlight constantly breaks down the methane in the atmosphere. *Huygens* showed that a layer of methane ice below the surface may turn into droplets and float into the atmosphere—as water does on Earth.

Cassini's radar could "see" through Titan's clouds to take this photo of a methane lake and rivers.

TITAN:
A WOW DISCOVERY

Like our planet, Titan has a rocky surface and rain that feeds rivers and lakes. But these bodies of liquid are like nothing seen on Earth!

Liquid world

Data from *Cassini* showed that more than 620,000 square miles of Titan's surface are covered in liquid—about 2 percent of the moon's total area. These lakes and seas are made of methane and ethane. The rest of Titan's surface has hills, valleys, and even some mountains. Some of these features have been carved by the liquid flowing across the surface.

Once *Huygens* landed, it photographed Titan's pebbly surface.

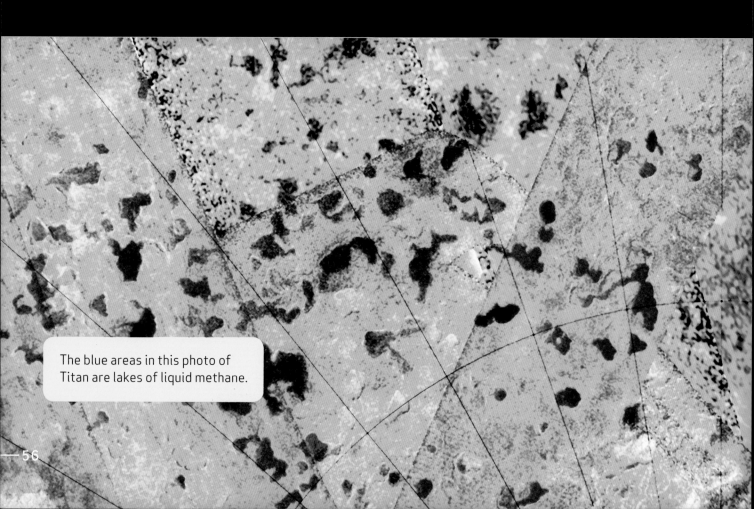

The blue areas in this photo of Titan are lakes of liquid methane.

BLUE GIANTS

The last two planets in the Solar System, Uranus and Neptune, are similar in many ways. These twin worlds are cold and icy—and blue!

One planet leads to another

Uranus was the first planet to be discovered using a telescope. The astronomer William Herschel spotted it in 1781, although he didn't realize right away that it was a planet. As astronomers tracked its orbit, they saw that it didn't travel exactly as expected. A French mathematician, Urbain Le Verrier, calculated that another large planet could be causing this. Astronomers soon found Neptune, right where Le Verrier had predicted it would be.

Uranus is slightly larger than Neptune, and paler in color.

URANUS

NEPTUNE

URANUS AND NEPTUNE:
A MISSION REPORT

9,000°F

THE TEMPERATURE OF URANUS' MANTLE, NEAR THE CORE

The spacecraft

Only one spacecraft has ever flown past Uranus and Neptune. *Voyager 2* passed Uranus in 1986, sending back photographs and data about the planet and its moons. Three years later, it flew within 3,000 miles of Neptune. Since then, we have used telescopes, such as the Hubble Space Telescope, to study these distant planets.

Uranus is surrounded by 13 faint rings, which were discovered in 1977.

What's inside the planets?

Both planets have a small, rocky core surrounded by an icy mantle made of water and ammonia. Near the core, this dense mantle gets very hot. Around the mantle is an outer layer of hydrogen and helium. There is also methane in the atmosphere, which gives both planets their blue color.

84 YEARS

THE AMOUNT OF TIME IT TAKES FOR URANUS TO COMPLETE ONE ORBIT OF THE SUN

Why is Uranus on its side?

Planets rotate around an imaginary line called an axis. With most planets, the axis is straight up and down, or slightly tilted, like Earth. Neptune's axis is tilted about as much as Earth's, but Uranus' axis is tilted so much that the planet spins on its side. Astronomers think that a huge impact long ago caused this

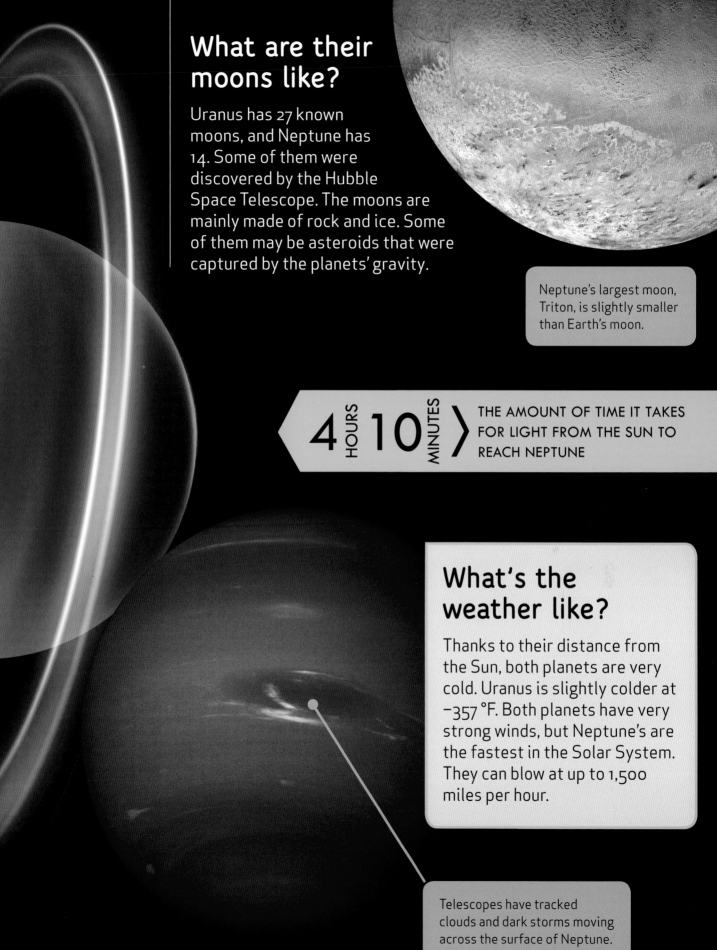

What are their moons like?

Uranus has 27 known moons, and Neptune has 14. Some of them were discovered by the Hubble Space Telescope. The moons are mainly made of rock and ice. Some of them may be asteroids that were captured by the planets' gravity.

Neptune's largest moon, Triton, is slightly smaller than Earth's moon.

4 HOURS 10 MINUTES ❯ THE AMOUNT OF TIME IT TAKES FOR LIGHT FROM THE SUN TO REACH NEPTUNE

What's the weather like?

Thanks to their distance from the Sun, both planets are very cold. Uranus is slightly colder at −357 °F. Both planets have very strong winds, but Neptune's are the fastest in the Solar System. They can blow at up to 1,500 miles per hour.

Telescopes have tracked clouds and dark storms moving across the surface of Neptune.

URANUS:
A WOW DISCOVERY

The Sun sends out a constant stream of charged particles. When they hit a planet, the results can be spectacular—and the Hubble Space Telescope has witnessed their effect on Uranus.

Amazing auroras

When charged particles come into contact with a planet's magnetic field, they are pushed into the upper atmosphere. There, they help create bursts of light called auroras. In 2011, Hubble became the first telescope to spot auroras on Uranus. A few years later, a team of astronomers used Hubble to see that the auroras rotate with the planet. They also discovered the location of Uranus' magnetic poles.

This Hubble photo shows an aurora at the bottom of the planet.

Auroras on Earth are caused by the same process that creates those on Uranus.

WATERY MOONS

Earth is the only planet in our Solar System with liquid water on its surface. Some moons also have water— but it is trapped beneath the surface.

Wonderful water

Water is necessary for all forms of life on Earth. It must flow as a liquid and not be frozen into ice. If life exists anywhere else in the Solar System, it's likely to be found on planets or moons that have liquid water. Jupiter's moon Ganymede has a rocky, icy crust with liquid water beneath. Another moon, Europa, has water under a crust of solid ice that is crisscrossed with cracks. Saturn's moon Enceladus shoots out fountains of ice crystals.

The red bands on Europa's icy surface are caused by salts.

MOONS:
A MISSION REPORT

The spacecraft

Most of what we know about these watery moons comes from *Galileo* and *Cassini*. In the 1990s, *Galileo* spent two years orbiting Jupiter to study its moons, before heading to Europa. *Cassini* performed dozens of flybys of Titan, Enceladus, and other moons of Saturn.

What is Europa made of?

Europa probably has an iron core and a rocky mantle, like Earth. Astronomers think that above the mantle is a giant ocean that covers the entire planet. The top layer is frozen solid to form a crust. *Galileo* took pictures of pits and domes in the icy crust. They may be a sign that warmer water below is changing the surface.

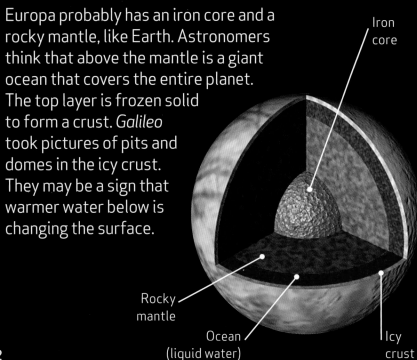

Iron core

Rocky mantle

Ocean (liquid water)

Icy crust

Is there water on Callisto?

Astronomers think that Callisto, one of Jupiter's moons, may also have an ocean beneath its surface. *Galileo* measured Callisto's magnetic field and found it changed in time with Jupiter's rotation. An ocean of salty water, which can carry electrical currents, could explain this.

EUROPA

CALLISTO

GANYMEDE

How can we "see" an underground ocean?

Astronomers can't see through Ganymede's icy, rocky crust. They use the Hubble Space Telescope to study the moon's auroras. They didn't match Jupiter's own auroras as closely as was expected. This makes astronomers think that a large ocean is affecting the magnetic fields.

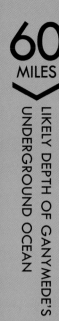

60 MILES

LIKELY DEPTH OF GANYMEDE'S UNDERGROUND OCEAN

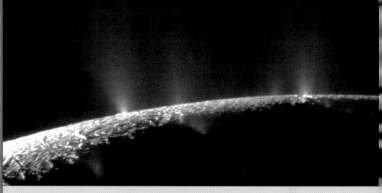

What's happening on Enceladus?

Saturn's moon Enceladus has an icy crust that reflects sunlight, making it very bright. In 2005, *Cassini* spotted that it is spewing out icy particles from geysers on the surface. The ice particles travel far from the moon, and they even supply material to one of Saturn's rings.

800 MPH

SPEED OF THE ICE GEYSERS ON ENCELADUS

ENCELADUS:
A WOW DISCOVERY

Astronomers knew there must be liquid water under the crust of Enceladus. In 2015, they realized there was a lot more water than they first thought.

Wobbly moon

The geysers on Enceladus were clustered around the south pole. *Cassini* took photos that showed that Enceladus wobbles slightly as it orbits. The wobble happens because the outer ice crust is not frozen solid. Astronomers realized there must be an ocean beneath the surface in that area.

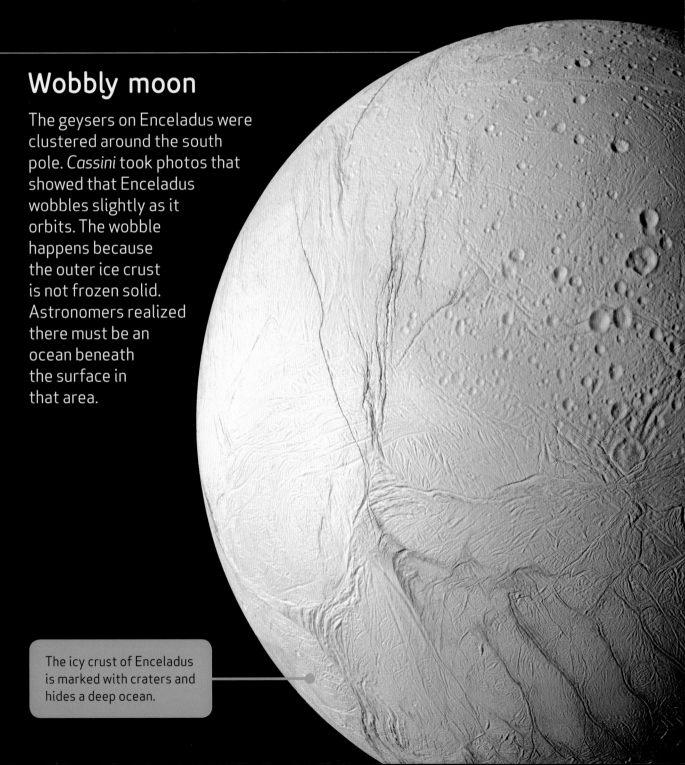

The icy crust of Enceladus is marked with craters and hides a deep ocean.

DWARF PLUTO

Tiny Pluto's orbit is billions of miles from the Sun, beyond Uranus and Neptune. It is one of several dwarf planets found in the outer Solar System.

Reinventing Pluto

Pluto was discovered in 1930, and for a long time it was listed as the ninth planet in the Solar System. However, in the 1990s astronomers discovered similar objects far out in the Solar System. One of them was even larger than Pluto. In 2006, astronomers around the world agreed on a new definition of a planet. Pluto was put into a new group—dwarf planets.

The name "Pluto" was suggested by an 11-year-old girl called Venetia Burney.

PLUTO:
A MISSION REPORT

The spacecraft

For years, we knew very little about Pluto. It wasn't until *New Horizons* arrived in 2015 that we learned more about this icy world. It took nearly ten years for the spacecraft to reach Pluto. When *New Horizons* was launched in 2006, Pluto was still known as a planet!

NEW HORIZONS

8,507 MILES ❯ SHORTEST DISTANCE BETWEEN *NEW HORIZONS* AND PLUTO

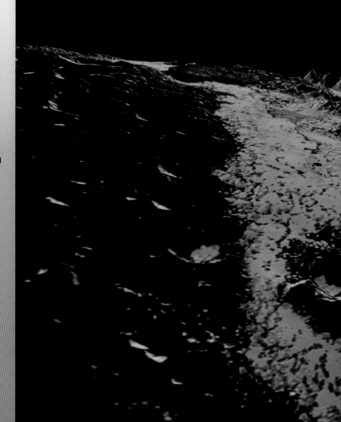

-391°F ❯ AVERAGE SURFACE TEMPERATURE ON PLUTO

What is a dwarf planet?

A dwarf planet is like a planet in two ways—it orbits a star, and it is big enough for its own gravity to pull it into a spherical shape. However, a planet's gravity is strong enough to clear other objects out of the path of its orbit. Dwarf planets like Pluto are not massive enough to do this.

248 YEARS TIME IT TAKES FOR PLUTO TO COMPLETE ONE ORBIT AROUND THE SUN

Pluto is so far away that before *New Horizons*, the best photos we had were fuzzy.

What is Pluto made of?

Pluto is part of a group of objects called the Kuiper Belt. They form a ring around the Sun, outside the orbit of Neptune. They are icy and rocky. Pluto probably has a rocky core, surrounded by a mantle made of ice. Its surface is covered in frozen gases such as nitrogen and methane.

CHARON

What's the surface like?

Pluto has craters and plains, as well as mountains. *New Horizons* discovered that the mountains are only about 100 million years old. Pluto's orbit is more of an oval than a circle, which means that sometimes it is much closer to the Sun than at other times. When it is close, frozen gases change from solid to gas and form a temporary atmosphere.

Pluto's surface has both bright, icy patches and dark, rugged land.

Does Pluto have moons?

Pluto has a large moon called Charon, which is almost half Pluto's size. *New Horizons* discovered a reddish patch at Charon's north pole that is the size of New Mexico. Pluto also has smaller moons called Nix, Hydra, Kerberos, and Styx.

PLUTO:
A WOW DISCOVERY

New Horizons took photos of Pluto, showing a huge light patch in the shape of a heart. This unusual feature turned out to be the largest glacier in the Solar System.

Heart of ice

The glacier is centered just above Pluto's equator. Astronomers have named it after Clyde Tombaugh, who discovered Pluto. Most of the ice that forms the heart is frozen nitrogen. The icy plains are split into smaller segments, separated by shallow troughs. There are also long dark streaks across the ice that may have been caused by wind.

The western half of the heart is named after *Sputnik*, the first satellite to orbit Earth.

There are mountains along some of the glacier's edges.

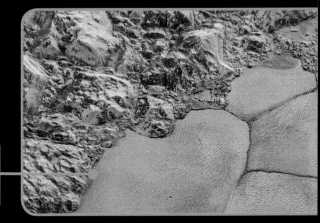

ICY COMETS

Every once in a while we get a visitor from the outer Solar System. Comets swoop by to loop around the Sun, with their magnificent tails streaming out.

Messengers of doom

People have observed comets for thousands of years. Their name comes from a Greek word meaning "long-haired," because of their tails. Until recently, people didn't know what comets really were. They were often seen as bad omens that predicted death or other disasters. Now we know they are small, icy objects that travel around the Sun.

Comet McNaught and its long tail lit up the skies for more than a week in 2007.

COMETS:
A MISSION REPORT

The spacecraft

Three spacecraft have made spectacular discoveries about comets. *Stardust* captured particles from a comet and returned them to Earth. *Deep Impact* caused a deliberate collision with a comet to study what was inside. In 2014, *Rosetta* became the first spacecraft to orbit a comet and to land a probe on it.

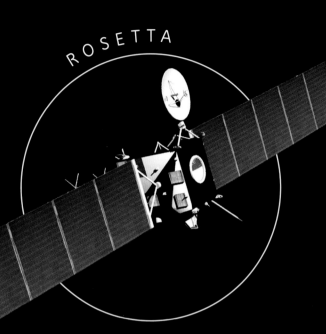

ROSETTA

3.73 MILES ⟩ DIAMETER OF COMET TEMPEL 1

What are comets made of?

The main body of a comet is called a nucleus. A nucleus is partly made of ice, but material captured by *Stardust* showed it also contains minerals from the hottest, innermost parts of the Solar System. *Deep Impact* found the nucleus of Comet Tempel 1 had areas of water ice beneath the surface.

Like most comets, Comet 67P is only a few miles across.

Where do comets come from?

Some comets come from the Kuiper Belt, and others come from an area called the Oort Cloud. The Oort Cloud is much farther away than the Kuiper Belt. In fact, it is about 100,000 times farther from the Sun than Earth. Comets from the Oort Cloud can take millions of years to complete one trip around the Sun.

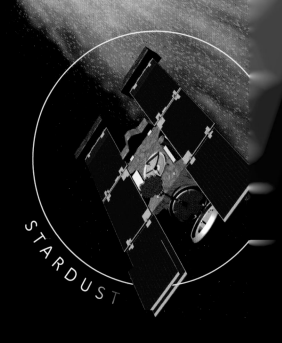

STARDUST

6.5 YEARS — AMOUNT OF TIME IT TAKES FOR COMET 67P TO ORBIT THE SUN

Comet Hale-Bopp was a bright comet spotted near Jupiter in 1995.

What's in a comet's tail?

When a comet gets close to the Sun, it heats up. Ice turns to gas and forms an enormous atmosphere called a coma. The force of the solar wind pushes on the coma. This turns some of its dust and gas into long tails. *Stardust* collected particles from the coma of Comet Wild 2 in 2004.

What's the surface like?

Rosetta provided the best close-up photos of the surface of a comet. During its two-year orbit of Comet 67P, it watched how the surface changed. As the comet heated up, cliffs collapsed, boulders moved across the surface, and cracks on the surface got longer.

Philae took this "selfie" once it came to rest on the surface of Comet 67P.

COMET 67P:
A WOW DISCOVERY

Many comets have crashed into Earth during its history. *Rosetta* showed that some of them may have brought very important chemicals with them.

Building blocks

Rosetta found several chemicals on Comet 67P that are necessary for life. It found phosphorus, an element found in all cells, and its lander, *Philae*, touched down on the comet's nucleus, where it found a type of simple sugar. Astronomers think comets may have brought materials like these to Earth, allowing life to develop.

Astronomers once thought Earth's water arrived when icy comets crashed into it. *Rosetta* found, however, that the water on some comets is different than on Earth.

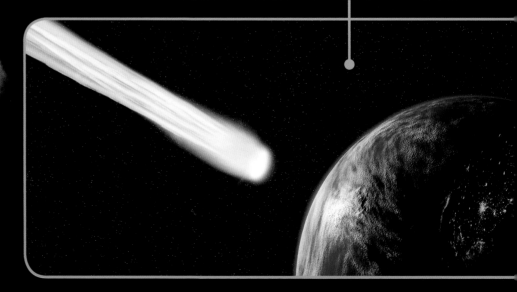

WHERE TO NEXT?

We have already discovered a lot about the Solar System. Astronomers are working on the next generation of spacecraft, which will help us learn even more.

Mining the moon

Space agencies and private companies are working on new landers, orbiters, and rovers to visit our closest neighbor—the Moon. Future missions will test new tools for mining the Moon or asteroids. These places have valuable resources, such as ice, helium, and rare metals. Helium can be used in nuclear power on Earth. Water could support colonies or be turned into rocket fuel.

Mission to Mars

To date, only robot spacecraft have visited Mars, but many groups would like to send astronauts there. NASA's *Mars 2020* mission will test a way of producing oxygen from Mars' atmosphere and map the locations of water and other resources. The information it sends back will help scientists plan ways for astronauts to land and live on Mars.

A colony on Mars would need sturdy buildings to protect people from dust storms and freezing temperatures.

How far can we go?

It takes several months to get to Mars, and astronauts would have to take all the food and supplies they needed for this long journey. Trips to Europa, Titan, or other faraway worlds would take even longer. At the moment, spacecraft carrying astronauts are just not capable of this. To visit these places, engineers will need to develop ways for bigger spacecraft to travel farther and faster, using less fuel.

Other Solar Systems

Billions of faraway stars are likely to have planets around them. These planets are called exoplanets, and astronomers have already discovered thousands of them. They use space telescopes, such as Kepler, to find them. Astronomers are hoping to find exoplanets with the right conditions for supporting life.

NASA is developing a new spacecraft called *Orion*, which will carry astronauts to the Moon, Mars, or even beyond.

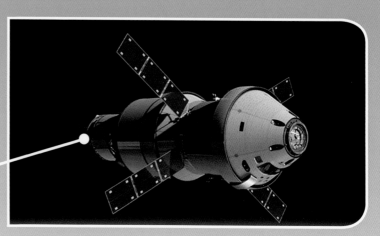

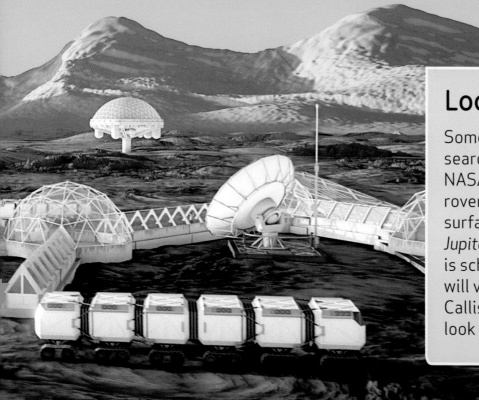

Looking for life

Some missions will continue the search for life on other worlds. NASA's *Mars 2020* and the *ExoMars* rover will drill into the red planet's surface to look for signs of life. *Jupiter Icy Moons Explorer* (*JUICE*) is scheduled to launch in 2022. It will visit Ganymede, Europa, and Callisto, to study their oceans and look for life.

MISSIONS THROUGH THE AGES

Name: *LANDSAT SATELLITES*
Launch dates: 1972, 1975, 1978, 1982, 1984, 1993, 1999, 2013
Target: Earth
Mission: To produce detailed maps of Earth

Name: *PIONEER 11*
Launch dates: 1973
Destination: Asteroid belt, Jupiter, Saturn
Mission: To explore the asteroid belt and learn more about Jupiter and Saturn

Name: *VOYAGER 2*
Launch date: 1977
Destination: Jupiter, Saturn, Uranus, Neptune, and the outer Solar System
Mission: To study the gas giant planets and explore the edges of the Solar System

Name: *GALILEO*
Launch date: 1989
Destination: Jupiter and its moons
Entered orbit: 1995
Mission: To study Jupiter and its rings and moons

Name: *MAGELLAN*
Launch date: 1989
Destination: Venus
Entered orbit: 1990
Mission: To create detailed images of Venus' rocky surface

Name: HUBBLE SPACE TELESCOPE
Launch date: 1990
Target: The Solar System and deep space
Mission: To take high-resolution images of objects in our Solar System and in deep space

Name: *CLEMENTINE*
Launch dates: 1994
Destination: Earth's Moon
Mission: To study the Moon and test new technologies

Name: *SOLAR AND HELIOSPHERIC OBSERVATORY (SOHO)*
Launch date: 1995
Target: The Sun
Mission: To study the Sun's layers

Name: *CASSINI-HUYGENS*
Launch date: 1997
Destination: Saturn and its moons
Entered Orbit: 2004
Huygens landing: 2005
Mission: To study the planet's atmosphere, magnetic field, moons, and rings

Name: *STARDUST*
Launch date: 1999
Destination: Annefrank (asteroid), Comet Wild 2, Comet Tempel 1
Mission: To collect samples of comet dust and return them to Earth

Name: *TERRA* (EARTH OBSERVING SYSTEM SATELLITE)
Launch date: 1999
Target: Earth
Mission: To study the impact of human activity on our planet

Name: *NEAR SHOEMAKER*
Launch date: 2000
Destination: Eros (asteroid)
Landed: 2001
Mission: To study a near-Earth asteroid

Name: *MESSENGER*
Launch date: 2004
Destination: Mercury
Entered Orbit: 2011
Mission: To study Mercury's geology and magnetic field

Name: *ROSETTA* AND *PHILAE*
Launch date: 2004
Destination: Comet 67P/
Churyumov-Gerasimenko
Entered orbit: 2014
Philae landing: 2014
Mission: To study a comet in detail
and land on its surface

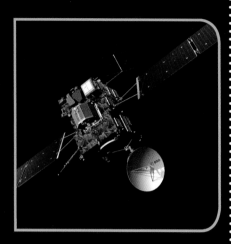

Name: *VENUS EXPRESS*
Launch date: 2005
Destination: Venus
Entered orbit: 2006
Mission: To study Venus'
atmosphere and weather

Name: *DEEP IMPACT*
Launch date: 2005
Destination: Comet Tempel 1,
Comet Hartley 2
Mission: To cause an impact with a
comet and study its composition

Name: *MARS RECONNAISSANCE
ORBITER*
Launch date: 2005
Destination: Mars
Entered orbit: 2006
Mission: To search for signs of
past water, study the Martian
weather, and look for future
landing sites

Name: *NEW HORIZONS*
Launch date: 2006
Destination: Pluto and the
Kuiper belt
Mission: To study Pluto and
another Kuiper belt object

Name: *DAWN*
Launch date: 2007
Destination: Vesta, Ceres
Entered orbit: 2011 (Vesta), 2015
(Ceres)
Mission: To learn more
about the formation of the
Solar System

Name: *CHANDRAYAAN-1*
Launch date: 2008
Destination: Earth's Moon
Entered orbit: 2008
Mission: To map the Moon and
test new technologies

Name: *LCROSS*
Launch date: 2009
Destination: Earth's Moon
Impact: 2009
Mission: To create an impact
at the Moon's pole to test for
water ice

Name: *LUNAR RECONNAISSANCE
ORBITER* (*LRO*)
Launch date: 2009
Destination: Earth's Moon
Entered orbit: 2009
Mission: To look for potential
landing sites and resources for
future missions

Name: *SOLAR DYNAMICS
OBSERVATORY* (*SDO*)
Launch date: 2010
Target: The Sun
Mission: To study how the
Sun changes and its influence
on Earth

Name: *SUOMI NPP*
Launch date: 2011
Target: Earth
Mission: To study
Earth's climate

Name: *CURIOSITY* (MARS
SCIENCE LABORATORY)
Launch date: 2011
Destination: Mars
Landed: 2012
Mission: To study Mars' geology
and climate and to look for signs
of water and life

Name: *JUNO*
Launch date: 2011
Destination: Jupiter
Entered orbit: 2016
Mission: To study Jupiter's core,
atmosphere, and magnetic field

Name: *MAVEN*
Launch date: 2013
Destination: Mars
Entered orbit: 2014
Mission: To study the planet's
atmosphere and the effects of the
solar wind

Name: *EXOMARS*
Launch date: 2016, with second
spacecraft planned to launch in
2020
Destination: Mars
Mission: To search for signs
of life and study gases in the
atmosphere

Name: *MARS 2020*
Planned Launch date: 2020
Destination: Mars
Mission: To look for signs of past
life and test technologies for
future crewed missions to Mars

Name: *JUPITER ICY MOONS
EXPLORER* (JUICE)
Planned Launch date: 2022
Destination: Ganymede, Europa,
and Callisto
Mission: To study their surfaces
and oceans and the possibility of
finding life there

GLOSSARY

Asteroid
Small, rocky body that orbits the Sun and is smaller than a planet or dwarf planet.

Astronomer
Person who studies planets, stars, and other objects in space.

Atmosphere
The layer of gases surrounding a planet or moon.

Atom
The smallest possible unit of matter.

Bacteria
Tiny living thing that has just one cell.

Carbon dioxide
A gas that is found in Earth's atmosphere and other places in space.

Comet
An icy object in space that travels in a long looping path around the Sun, forming a long, bright tail as it heats up.

Core
The center area of something, such as a planet or moon.

Crater
A hollow area, like the inside of a bowl, created when an object crashes into a planet or other large object.

Crust
Thin outer layer of a planet or other object.

Dwarf planet
An object in the Solar System that is not big enough, or does not have strong enough gravity, to be considered a planet.

Eclipse
When one object in space temporarily blocks the view of another object.

Flyby
A mission in which a spacecraft flies past a planet or other object and studies it on the way.

Galaxy
A group of billions of stars and other objects held together by gravity.

Glacier
A large mass of ice that moves very slowly across land.

Gravity
The force that pulls all objects toward each other.

Lander
A spacecraft designed to touch down on a planet, asteroid, or other object.

Magnetic field
The space around an object in which a magnetic force is active.

Mantle
The layer of some planets and other objects that is between the crust and the core.

Mass
A measure of how much matter is in an object.

Methane
Gas that is found on Earth and some other planets and moons.

Moon
An object that orbits a planet, dwarf planet, or asteroid.

Orbit
The path an object takes around a larger object; or, to travel on this path.

Orbiter
A spacecraft designed to go into orbit around a planet or other object and study it.

Planet
A large object that orbits a star, with nothing else in its path.

Pole
One end of an imaginary line through the center of a planet or space object.

Radar
The use of radio waves to study faraway objects. Waves are sent out and then picked up again when they bounce back after hitting an object.

Radiation
Waves of energy sent out by a source such as the Sun.

Rotate
To spin around a central axis. The rotation of Earth is what creates night and day.

Rover
A robot vehicle that travels across the surface of a planet or moon and collects data.

Satellite
An object that moves around another object. A satellite can be natural, such as a moon, or it can be artificial, such as a spacecraft.

Solar flare
A short, intense burst of gases coming out of the Sun.

Solar wind
A stream of electrified gas that flies out of the Sun and across space at a very high speed.

Spherical
Round, like a ball shape.

Sunspot
A dark patch that sometimes appears on the Sun's surface.

INDEX